THE
SILENT SPARK
Level Up Your Potential

CHIP KENDALL

Sarah Grace Publishing
Dyslexic Friendly

an imprint of
malcolm down
PUBLISHING

LEVEL UP
BOOKS

Copyright © 2025 Chip Kendall

First published 2025 by Grace and Down Publishing Ltd
an imprint of Malcolm Down Publishing
www.malcolmdown.co.uk

28 27 26 25   6 5 4 3 2 1

British Library Cataloguing in Publication Data
A catalogue record for this book is available from the
British Library.

ISBN 978-1-917455-27-5 *The Silent Spark – Level Up
Your Potential*

Cover design and illustrations by Hannah Joy Williams
Art direction by Sarah Grace
Level Up Logo Design by Joe Dunys

Printed in the UK

ENDORSEMENTS

"This is a much needed series which will empower, validate and encourage a generation of children and families. It's inspiringly full of fun, faith & facts. I can't wait to read it with my daughter!"

Gemma Hunt, CBeebies Presenter and Author

"This punchy, pithy, and power-packed book is a brilliant call to action for the rising generation. It inspires kids to recognise their God-given potential, step out with confidence, and partner with Jesus to bring light, life, and love to the world around them. Every page champions creativity, courage, and the truth that every child is made on purpose for a purpose."

Matt Summerfield, Senior Leader at Zeo Church and Board of Trustees at Youthscape

"Level Up is exactly the kind of resource today's precious young minds need. In a world that often overwhelms or distracts, these books invite curiosity, build confidence, and encourage character, all at the very age when the brilliant brain is most open to growth.

Thanks to the incredible gift of neuroplasticity, this season of life is uniquely wired for shaping thought patterns, exploring potential, and building a sense of identity that lasts. Chip's voice is fun, and wise meeting readers where they are at whilst calling them higher. Level Up isn't just a book series, it's a toolkit for life, guiding young people to see themselves and their world with fresh eyes."

Jo Hargreaves, The Faith Filled Therapist

As a Christian Headteacher, I can say without hesitation that these books are both timely and much needed. Chip has an incredible gift for communicating the gospel of hope and love in a way that truly connects with children. I believe these books—and the message they carry—are essential for every Christian school and home.

Neil Garratt, Headteacher, Elworth Church of England Primary School

The Level Up series is needed for all children to reach their full potential and discover their true value. Chip breaks down each concept into an accessible way for children to grasp and then run with for life. Full of quotes from famous people, thought provoking stories and inspiring tales this series will encourage children to aspire to more as they engage with this thought-provoking series.

Olly Goldenberg, Children Can

"Chip has done it again! Level Up is full of encouragement, wisdom and joy—jam-packed with tools to help children know who they are, Whose they are, and how to be light in the world around them.

As a mum, I want my kids to read it. As a children's ministry leader, I want every child I know to read it.

This series will fire up imaginations, strengthen hearts, and point a generation towards Jesus in the most fun and faith-filled way. Absolutely brilliant!"

Shell Perris, ALIVE Kids

This resource does exactly what it promises—it takes us up a level! It's a permission-giving laboratory where new possibilities can grow.

It's a playground where kids can learn by doing and encounter God through joy and play. It's a Chip meal on a plate—loaded with extra, unique flavours!

It's also a wake-up call to the Church, parents, and adults everywhere to inspire our kids to become world-changers. This resource deserves to go viral.

Above all, it's a training manual to help young lives live and thrive in God's unshakeable Kingdom—especially when everything around us feels shaky.

Thank you, Chip, for your love and obedience in creating this series. Church—let's wake up and level up!

Andy Kennedy, King's Kids International

Fantastic insights and practical steps to developing life giving character traits that lead to fulfilment and blessings. Illuminated by great stories and inspiration from the lives of wonderful role models.

Dom Conidi – Scripture Union England and Wales

Chip Kendall is a vibrant communicator whose energy, vision and passion shine through his writing. The Level Up series is packed full of inspiration and written in a way that will help young people grow in confidence and character.

The world we inhabit needs young people who can lead with purpose and passion and this series will equip and resource a new generation to become the change they want to see.

Andy Wolfe, Executive Director of Education, National Society for Education (Church of England & Church in Wales)

"Full of inspiration and encouragement for young minds. I love how it makes faith real and relevant."

Sam Hailes, Editor, Premier Christianity magazine

DEDICATION

For Helen — beautiful, wise and the love
of my life. For such an impatient person,
you're certainly very patient with me.

THANK YOU

This series wouldn't exist without a whole team of legends behind the scenes, and I want to take a moment to say a massive thank you to each one of you.

To my amazing wife, **Helen** — thank you for being willing to take the plunge with me and cheer this whole project into existence. Your faith, courage and partnership mean the world.

To **Katherine**, my brilliant sister-in-law — your early research laid the tracks before the train had even left the station. Thank you for believing in this idea from the very beginning.

To **Hannah**, your stunning illustrations and creative design ideas have brought these pages to life in ways I couldn't have imagined. You've captured the heart of Level Up in every line and colour.

To **Malcolm**, **Sarah**, **Lydia** and the whole team at Grace Down — thank you for your skill, patience and professionalism, turning words and pictures into books that kids will actually want to pick up and read.

To Pastor **Glyn**, thank you for writing such powerful forewords and always championing the next generation with such passion and purpose.

To **Gemma**, your endorsement was the fuel I didn't know I needed — thank you for your encouragement and support.

To **Joe**, thanks for such a fun logo. You smashed it out the park.

To my kids, my family, and my friends — thanks for being the inspiration, the sounding boards, and the spark that keeps me going.

And finally, to every headteacher and teacher I've ever had the privilege of working with — thank you for opening your doors and hearts to this vision of investing in the next generation. Your daily courage and care are heroic.

To every young person reading these books: I'm praying you grow in wisdom, stature and favour with God and with people. You've got this — because He's got you.

Stay bold. Stay curious. Stay kind.

— Chip

CONTENTS

FOREWORD
by Glyn Barrett

Some of the brightest flames start with the tiniest spark.

You might not feel impressive. Maybe you're not the loudest in the room, the fastest on the pitch or the one always putting their hand up in class. But let me tell you something I've learned over the years: potential doesn't always shout. Sometimes it whispers. Sometimes it hides. Sometimes it shows up in unexpected ways and surprises everyone, including you.

But it's there.

In The Silent Spark, Chip Kendall unpacks one of the greatest truths every young person needs to hear: you are carrying something incredible inside you. It might not be evident to others yet, and maybe not even to yourself, but that doesn't mean it's not real. God has placed purpose, passion and power inside every person, and this book will help you dig it up, dust it off and let it shine.

I love that this book doesn't just hype kids up for five minutes. It builds. It challenges. It stretches. It shows that your potential isn't something that magically appears overnight; it's something you grow into, with faith, courage and a little bit of grit. As Ephesians 2:10 says, "For we are God's handiwork, created in Christ Jesus to do good works, which God prepared in advance for us to do."

And here's the kicker: that spark in you? It's not just for you. It's for the world around you. For the lives you'll touch, the problems you'll help solve, the creativity you'll unleash, the justice you'll fight for. Whether you dream of building businesses, writing songs, leading teams, or simply being the kind of person others can count on, you've got a spark. And it matters.

Chip's writing has this brilliant way of mixing profound truth with fun stories and down-to-earth wisdom. He'll make you laugh one minute and reflect the next. And by the end of this book, I believe every reader will walk a little taller – because when you discover your potential, you can't help but live purposefully.

So here's my prayer for you: may this book fan your silent spark into a roaring flame. May you see yourself the way God sees you. And may your journey of discovering your potential be just the beginning of something world-changing.

Let's Level Up.

Glyn Barrett
Senior Pastor, !Audacious Church
National Leader, Assemblies of God Great Britain

INTRODUCTION

You were made to shine.

Somewhere deep inside you, there's a spark. It's small, but it's powerful. It's the spark of *potential* – everything you could become, do, imagine and create. You might not see it yet. But it's there, just waiting for the right moment to light up.

When you learn something new, try something brave, or dream big – you're feeding that spark. And here's the best part: your spark was placed there on purpose, by the One who made you. God created you with amazing potential, and He's ready to help you shine.

This book will help you find that spark, grow it and share it with the world. Each chapter is packed with real stories, mind-blowing facts from nature, fun challenges, and Bible truth to help you discover:

- What's inside you
- Why it matters
- And how to let it shine.

Are you ready?
Let's find your spark.

CHAPTER ONE

LIGHT THE FUSE
Potential to...succeed

> "Potential is a priceless treasure, like gold. All of us have gold hidden within, but we have to dig to get it out."

Joyce Meyer, author

Jono was hungry.

"Mum, is there anything I can eat?" he shouted upstairs.

His mother's reply was kind yet firm. "You've already eaten two slices of toast since you got home from school, honey."

"I know, but I'm still hungry. How long is it until dinner?" he asked.

"Two hours. Why don't you chop up a piece of fruit for yourself?" she answered.

Jono thought this was a great idea, and after eating a couple of kiwi fruits, he felt much better. An hour or so later, he decided he'd help his mum prepare dinner.

"Mum, why are there some parts of the day when I feel so much hungrier than others?" he asked. "Is it because I'm not eating enough at meal times?"

"Not necessarily," she replied. "Do you know what your metabolism is?"

"No," Jono answered. "Sounds like something to do with science though."

"Yes, that's right," his mum answered. "It's your body's process of turning food into energy. You need energy for everything – moving, thinking, growing – and at your age, you're doing quite a lot of all those things. So it's only natural that you're going to be hungry a lot of the time."

"I guess that makes sense."

After a few moments, his mum carried on, "You know, honey, it is possible to be hungry for more than just food."

"What do you mean?" Jono asked.

"In the same way your metabolism turns food into energy, you've got the potential to turn your hunger for *learning* into the power to succeed."

What is Potential?

Potential basically means having the ability to develop, achieve or succeed. It comes from the Latin word *potentia* meaning *power*, *strength* and *force*. *Potentia* is also the root for the word *potency* which is used to describe just how powerful something really is.

A bird has the potential to fly.

A lion has the potential to roar.

An athlete has the potential to win.

And you have the potential to be *great*.

In this book, we're going to explore what it means to develop our potential to succeed, grow, learn, build, create and change. But before we really get into it, think about the people in your world who are shining examples of reaching their potential to succeed.

Who do you see as being successful?

....

....

....

....

Who has used the power they have to achieve something great?

....

....

....

....

Who has changed the way you see the world?

....

....

....

....

The Key to Success

In order to reach your full potential, it is important to remember that success doesn't happen overnight. We live in a world where it is normal to buy fast food, receive same-day deliveries, and get thousands of likes within minutes on social media. If we're not careful, we can start to think that we have somehow evolved as the human race, and we no longer need to do any hard work.

But, actually, the opposite is true. In many ways, hard work is the *key* to success. We may be tempted to give up the first time we fail, but the reality is that we must be prepared to fail multiple times before we achieve any type of success in any area of our lives. Failure is not final. It is just another opportunity to dust ourselves off, learn how NOT to do something, and then give it another go. That takes courage. That's the key to success.

GOLDFISH

A relatively small member of the carp family, goldfish can reach immense sizes if given the opportunity. Everyone who ever owned a goldfish probably knows that the only thing that limits a goldfish's growth is its container. If kept in a small aquarium, goldfish typically only grow to 3–6 centimetres long. However, when raised in large tanks or ponds, goldish can reach sizes between 35 and 45 centimetres long. While most goldfish live between 10 to 15 years, some can live over 40 years, which extends their growth potential. In addition to changing sizes, goldfish can also change colours. If left in a dark space, they will slowly change from an orangish-red colour to grey or white. This happens because the pigments in a goldfish's cells reflect light and give it colour. When kept from light, their skin changes over time and eventually loses colouration.

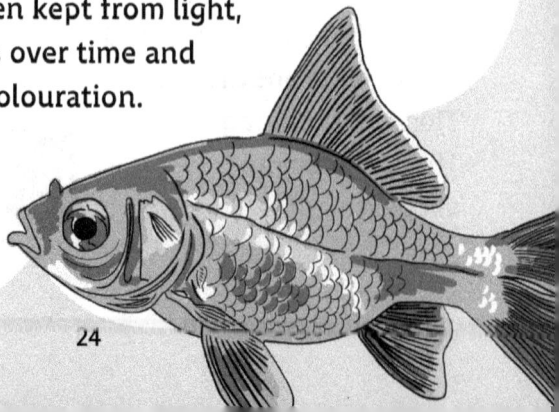

CHAPTER TWO

FAN THE FLAME
Potential to...grow

"It is exactly in tough times when we discover our full potential, it allows our mind and body to push ourselves beyond our limits."

Leonardo Bonucci, Italian footballer

Esther was tired.

"Dad, can you get me a pen, please?"

Her father looked up from his laptop and replied, "Sweetie, they're in the drawer right behind you."

"I know, but I'm so tired right now that I can't be bothered to turn around."

Her father had a little giggle to himself. This was starting to become a regular occurrence ever since Esther started her small baking business. Most of her energy was already spent by the time she sat down to do her homework.

Patiently, he closed his laptop, retrieved the pen, and gave it to her along with a little hug. "You're doing a great job, sweetie. Don't give up. All healthy things need time and space to grow."

"Thanks, Dad. But what do you mean by 'grow'? What does gardening have to do with me being tired?" she asked.

"Ha-ha, fair enough," he said. "Think about it – you're a lot like a plant right now. You're growing physically, mentally, emotionally and even professionally with your new cake business. Doesn't it make perfect sense that you're going to feel a little bit tired?"

Esther was starting to follow his train of thought. "Wow, I hadn't thought of it like that. I suppose you're right. But why does baking seem to *give* me energy and homework seems to *drain* it so much?"

"Oh, that's easy," he replied. "It's because of the season you're in right now."

Esther was enjoying the idea of being like a plant. "Seasons? Like winter and spring?" She spread out her arms like she was a giant sunflower.

Her dad grinned widely. "Exactly! You're in a season of life where baking is fun and homework feels like a chore. But believe it or not, in a few years' time you may find the exact opposite is true – your work feels satisfying and baking feels like a chore. The main thing is that you take each season as it comes, and allow yourself plenty of time and space to never stop growing."

Healthy Things Grow

Have you ever stopped to consider how amazing it is that things grow at different speeds? A pineapple takes between 2–3 years to grow, but a mango can grow in just 3–6 months. A watermelon (the biggest of all of them) can grow even quicker than 3 months.

It's the same with animals. A baby fox is in its mum's womb for around 2 months, while a baby goat spends around 5 months growing in the womb. Much bigger animals like giraffes and elephants are in their mums' tummies for nearly two years! That's a lot of growing.

Despite how long it may take, the fact remains that all healthy things grow – including us as people. And I'm not just talking about our physical bodies.

Our minds grow in knowledge.

Our ideas grow in ambition.

Our hearts grow in love and compassion.

And our hopes grow to make the world a better place.

Let's take a moment to consider our own growth potential. Think about what your life was like just one year ago.

How much taller am I? How many clothes have I grown out of?

....
....
....
....

What were my biggest challenges and goals then? What are they now?

....
....
....
....

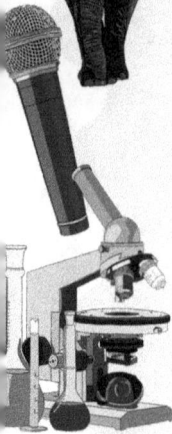

What extra responsibilities have I taken on recently? How might they help me to grow?

....
....
....
....

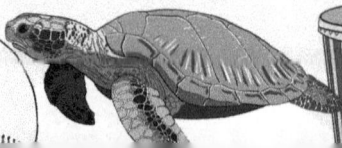

A Lesson from the Chinese Bamboo Tree

Like any plant, the Chinese bamboo tree requires nurturing – water, fertile soil, sunshine – in order to flourish properly. Interestingly, in the first year there are no visible signs of activity or development. In the second year, again, no growth above the soil. And the third and fourth, still no signs. Patience is tested, and we begin to wonder if our efforts will ever be rewarded. But finally, in the fifth year – bam! There is growth, and a LOT of it! The Chinese bamboo tree grows nearly 30 metres tall in just six weeks.

The lesson we learn from the Chinese bamboo tree is that even though our potential isn't always easy to see, it is definitely still there. Beneath the surface of our lives, the hard work and tough times are always paying off. When the time is right, we'll grow even quicker than we realised, and others will notice too.

CHAPTER THREE

FUEL THE FIRE
Potential to...learn

> "One has to remember that every failure can be a stepping stone to something better."

Colonel Sanders, founder of KFC

Liam was frustrated.

"Ugh! I just don't get it!" he exclaimed, tossing his pencil onto his notebook. "No matter how many times I try, I just don't understand these equations."

His older sister, Mia, looked up from her own work. "What are you working on?"

"Maths," Liam groaned. "I keep making mistakes, and it's so annoying."

Mia smiled sympathetically. "I get it. Learning new things can be tough. But you know what? Mistakes aren't a bad thing."

"How?" Liam asked. "They just make me feel like I'm failing."

"Well," Mia said, "think of mistakes like stepping stones. Each one brings you closer to figuring things out. You remember when you were learning to ride your bike? You fell a bunch of times but, each time, you got better at balancing. Learning anything is the same – it takes practice, patience and sometimes a little bit of struggle. But every time you do something wrong you just learn another way of how NOT to do it."

Liam sighed. "So, you're saying if I keep making mistakes, I'll eventually get it?"

"Exactly," Mia nodded. "As long as you learn from them and keep trying, you're always improving. That's the whole point of learning!"

The Power of Learning

Learning is one of the most important ways we can develop our potential. It's how we grow, adapt and become better versions of ourselves. But real learning isn't just about memorising facts or passing tests – it's about gaining new skills, understanding new ideas and discovering new possibilities.

Think about some of the greatest minds in history. They didn't start out as geniuses. They had to learn, struggle and make mistakes along the way.

- **Thomas Edison**, the inventor of the light bulb, failed thousands of times before he succeeded.

- **Albert Einstein** wasn't considered a top student when he was young, but he went on to change the way we understand the universe.

- **Serena Williams** didn't win every tennis match when she started but, through training and learning, she became one of the greatest athletes in history.

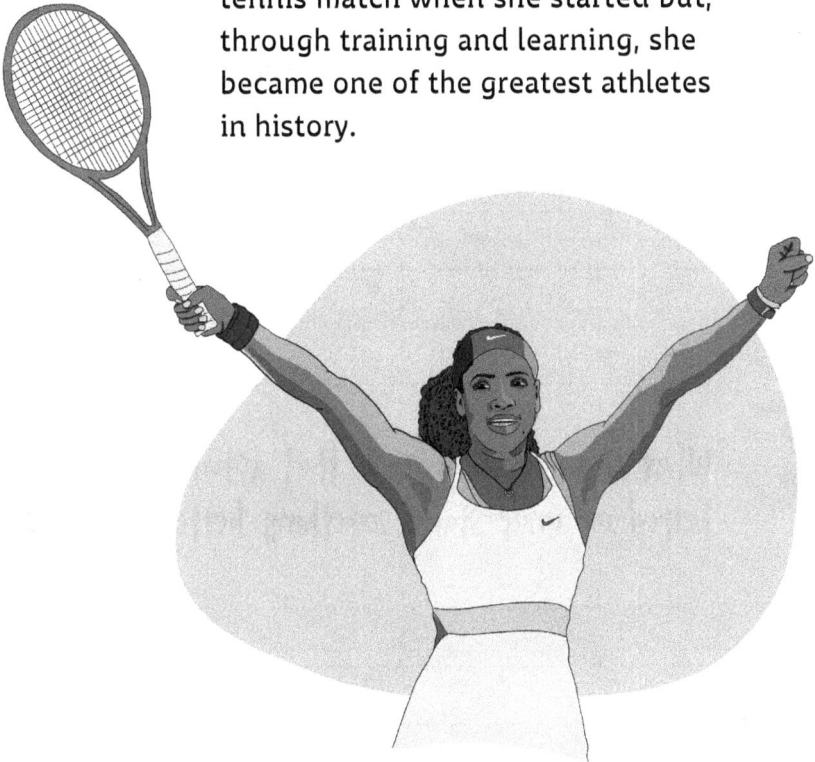

If these people had given up, the world would be a very different place. Learning isn't about being perfect – it's about making progress.

Take a moment to think about the ways you've learned and grown recently.

What is something new I've learned this year?

....

....

....

....

What is a mistake I made that actually helped me understand something better?

....

....

....

....

What is something I'd love to learn in the future?

....

....

....

....

A Lesson from the Wright Brothers

The Wright brothers, Orville and Wilbur, had a dream
– to build a machine that could fly. But in the early
1900s, most people thought that was impossible. The
brothers spent years studying, testing and making
mistakes. Their first designs didn't work and they
crashed many times. But instead of giving up, they

used each failure as a lesson. They adjusted their designs, learned more about aerodynamics, and kept improving.

Finally, in 1903, they achieved their goal. The Wright brothers made history by flying the first powered aeroplane. Their ability to learn from mistakes and keep going changed the world forever.

The lesson we learn from them? Learning isn't always easy, but it's always worth it. Every mistake, every challenge and every bit of effort adds up to something greater in the end.

So the next time you feel frustrated while learning something new, remember – you have the potential to grow, improve and succeed. All you have to do is keep going.

THE HUMAN BRAIN

Our brains always have the capacity to learn. The brain continues to change constantly with learning and experience throughout all of life and never becomes fixed and unchanging. Therefore, someone's "smartness" is as much about their brain connectivity from learning, not just about their biology.

Learning is essentially something that the brain just does automatically. As we experience different situations in our everyday life, carry out our day-to-day tasks, encounter problems and find solutions, those pathways used in our brain most frequently strengthen their connections, forming habits, reinforcing memories and improving skills. Of course, learning can also be deliberate, when we practise or train, but the same principles of changing and strengthening connections apply whenever those pathways are used.

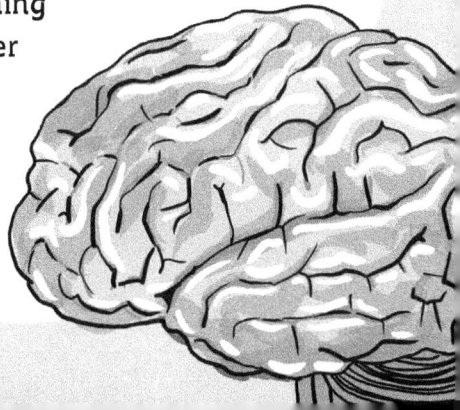

DEEP DIVE:
George Washington Carver

The Man Who Saw Potential in a Peanut

George Washington Carver was born into a world where people like him – black children born into slavery – were often told they had no future. But Carver refused to believe that. Instead, he looked at the world around him and saw **potential** – even in the most ordinary things.

A Difficult Start in Life

George was born during a time when slavery still existed in America. He, his mother and his sister were kidnapped when he was just a baby. His owner, Moses Carver, searched for them but only found George.

After slavery was abolished, Moses and his wife Susan raised George and his brother James as their own children. They encouraged George to learn, and he loved discovering new things. But life wasn't easy – black children weren't allowed to attend the local school, so George had to walk **10 miles** just to find a school where he was welcome. He was so determined to learn that when he arrived and found the school closed, he **slept in a barn** just so he could be there for lessons the next morning!

A Prayer and a Peanut

As George grew older, he never stopped being curious. He loved plants and science, so he worked hard to become a teacher and inventor. Eventually, he became a scientist at **Tuskegee Institute**, where he studied ways to help farmers grow better crops.

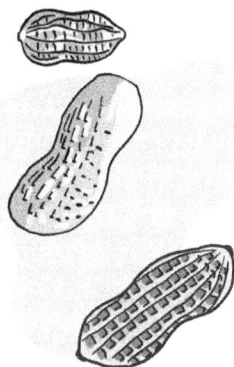

At the time, many farmers in the southern United States grew cotton, but cotton was ruining the soil. Carver encouraged them to plant peanuts instead because peanuts **put nutrients back into the soil**. But there was a problem – no one knew what to do with all those peanuts!

So, Carver prayed:

"Dear Lord, why did You make the peanut?"

He believed that if he asked God, He would show him the potential hidden inside this small, ordinary nut.

Unlocking Potential

God answered his prayer. Carver discovered **over 300 uses for the peanut!** He found ways to turn peanuts into **peanut oil, peanut soap, peanut glue, peanut rubber, peanut ink and even peanut shampoo!**

Many people think George Washington Carver invented peanut butter, but it actually existed before his time! However, his work with peanuts helped make them one of the most useful and valuable crops in the world.

One of his biggest moments came in **1921**, when he was invited to speak before the U.S. Congress about his discoveries. At first, the people in charge gave him **just 10 minutes** to talk. But when they heard what he had to say, they were so amazed that they let him speak for **an hour and forty-five minutes!**

When one congressman asked how he had learned so much, Carver simply said:

"From an old book."

"What book?" the man asked.

"The Bible," Carver replied.

"Does the Bible talk about peanuts?"

Carver smiled and said, **"No, but it tells about the God who made the peanut. I asked Him to show me what to do with the peanut, and He did."**

More Than Just Peanuts

Carver became one of the most respected scientists in the world, not just because of what he invented, but because of how he lived. He could have made a fortune from his discoveries, but he chose not to **patent most of his ideas** – he wanted them to be available to **help as many people as possible.**

He once said, **"The Lord has guided me, and without my Saviour, I am nothing."**

Carver also believed that science and faith went hand in hand. He saw **God's hand in everything**, from the trees to the tiniest plants, and he encouraged young people to **ask God for wisdom** in their own lives.

What Can We Learn from George Washington Carver?

- **Potential is everywhere!** Even something as small as a peanut can change the world if we look at it with curiosity and creativity.

- **Faith and science can work together.** Carver believed that asking God for guidance led him to his greatest discoveries.

- **True success is about helping others.** Carver didn't keep his discoveries to himself – he shared them so that farmers, families and communities could have a better future.

A Final Thought

Carver once said, **"Start where you are, with what you have. Make something of it and never be satisfied."**

He proved that **potential** isn't about where you come from – it's about what you choose to do with the gifts God has given you.

What small thing in your life might have **big potential** waiting to be discovered?

CHAPTER FOUR

BURNING BRIGHTER
Potential to...build

"Focusing your life solely on making
a buck shows a certain poverty
of ambition. It asks too little of
yourself. Because it's only when
you hitch your wagon to something
larger than yourself that you realise
your true potential."

Barack Obama, former president of the USA

Ethan was uncertain.

His hands hovered over the pile of wooden planks in front of him. "I don't think I can do this, Mr Carter," he admitted.

His teacher, Mr Carter, knelt down beside him. "Of course you can. Building something new always feels tricky at first, but that's part of the process."

Ethan sighed. "What if I mess up?"

Mr Carter smiled. "Then you'll learn. Think of building like solving a puzzle – you start with small pieces, fit them together and, little by little, you create something amazing. Every great builder started as a beginner. And remember, most of the things we build today are based on the work of those who came before us."

Ethan hesitated, then picked up a hammer. "Okay ... I'll give it a shot."

The Importance of Building

Building isn't just about creating something physical – it's about constructing ideas, relationships and even our own future. Whether it's a house, a business or a dream, everything great starts with small steps and determination.

Consider some of the most well-known builders in history:

- The ancient Egyptians built the pyramids, one block at a time.

- Engineers and architects design skyscrapers that touch the sky.

- Innovators like Steve Jobs and Elon Musk built companies that changed the world.

But none of these people built from nothing. They stood on the shoulders of those who came before them, learning from past ideas and improving on them. We all have the opportunity to build upon what others have started.

Now, think about your own life.

What is something I have built recently (a project, a friendship, a new habit)?

....

....

....

....

What is something I want to build in the future?

....

....

....

....

What steps can I take to start building today?

....

....

....

....

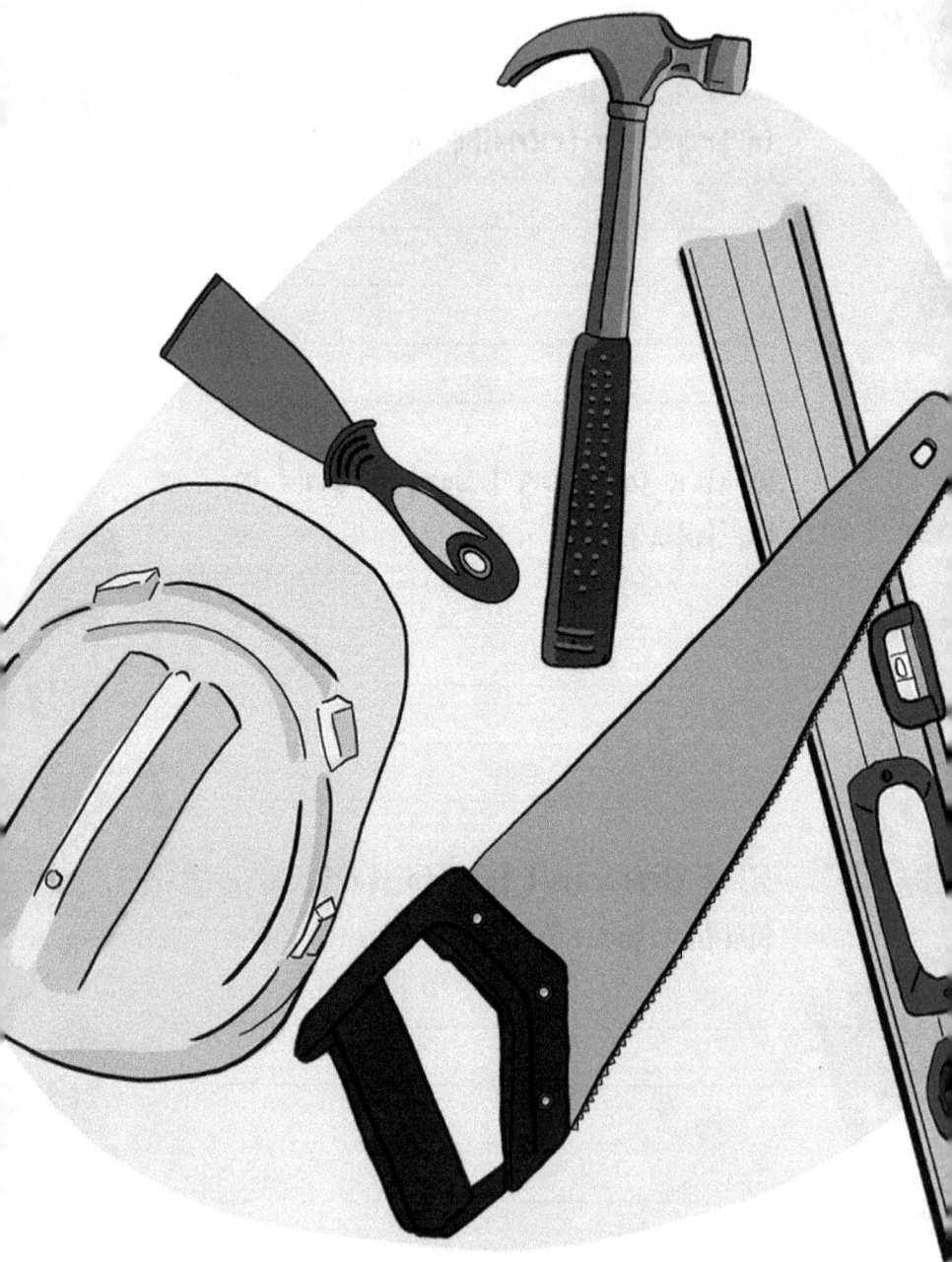

A Lesson from the Three Little Pigs and the Wise Builder

The classic story of the Three Little Pigs teaches us a valuable lesson about building. The first two pigs built their homes quickly out of straw and sticks, but when the big bad wolf came, their houses collapsed. The third pig, however, took his time and built a strong house out of bricks. When the wolf tried to blow it down, the house stood firm.

Jesus shared a similar lesson in the Bible. He told a parable about two builders: one who built his house on sand and another who built on solid rock. When the storms came, the house on the sand collapsed, but the house on the rock stood strong. The message? A strong foundation makes all the difference.

The lesson? Anything worth building takes effort, patience and strong foundations. Whether it's a skill, a career or a dream, the best things in life aren't rushed – they're built with care and persistence.

So don't be afraid to start building. One step at a time, you'll create something great.

BEAVERS

Beavers have earned the nickname "Nature's Engineers" for their amazing ability to build a dam that is completely watertight in under 24 hours. They dam an area, flood it, and end up providing necessary habitat for shorebirds, waterfowl, drinking water for mammals, soil for aquatic plant life, expanded areas for fish to feed, and incredible rebirth in lands that really need it.

CHAPTER FIVE

FIND THE SPARK
Potential to...create

"I like to think of ideas as potential energy. They're really wonderful, but nothing will happen until we risk putting them into action."

Mae Jemison, American astronaut and first black woman in space

Ava was inspired.

"Alright, everyone, let's try that again, but this time I want you to really feel the music!" Mrs Daniels, the choir leader, encouraged.

The choir sang, their voices blending beautifully. When it was Ava's turn for her solo, she sang it with a little twist – adding a slight variation to the melody. She hadn't planned to do it, but it just felt right in the moment.

Mrs Daniels raised an eyebrow but smiled warmly. When the song ended, she clapped her hands. "That was wonderful, everyone! And Ava, I noticed you made a small change to your solo. Tell me about that."

Ava hesitated. "I'm sorry, Mrs Daniels. I didn't mean to change it. It just sort of happened."

"Never apologise for creativity," Mrs Daniels said with a grin. "Music is alive. It breathes, it moves and, sometimes, it surprises us. That was a beautiful touch, Ava. Keep exercising your potential to create."

Ava beamed. "Really? So it's okay to make little changes?"

"Of course," Mrs Daniels replied. "That's how new songs are written, and how musicians find their unique sound. Creativity is a gift – and you, my dear, have plenty of it."

Ava felt a warmth spread in her chest. She never thought of herself as particularly creative, but maybe she had more potential than she realised.

The Power of Creativity

Creativity is more than just painting a picture or writing a song. It's about seeing the world in a new way, thinking outside the box, and coming up with ideas that didn't exist before. Creativity is what allows scientists to make discoveries, engineers to build new inventions, and storytellers to create whole new worlds.

Think about some of the most creative minds in history:

- **Leonardo da Vinci** imagined flying machines long before aeroplanes existed.

- **Marie Curie** discovered radium and changed the way we understand science.

- **Lin-Manuel Miranda** combined history and hip-hop to create *Hamilton*, one of the most ground-breaking musicals of our time.

- **J.K. Rowling** built an entire magical universe in her mind before writing it down.

The world is shaped by people who dare to create. You have that same potential inside you!

Take a moment to reflect on your own creativity:

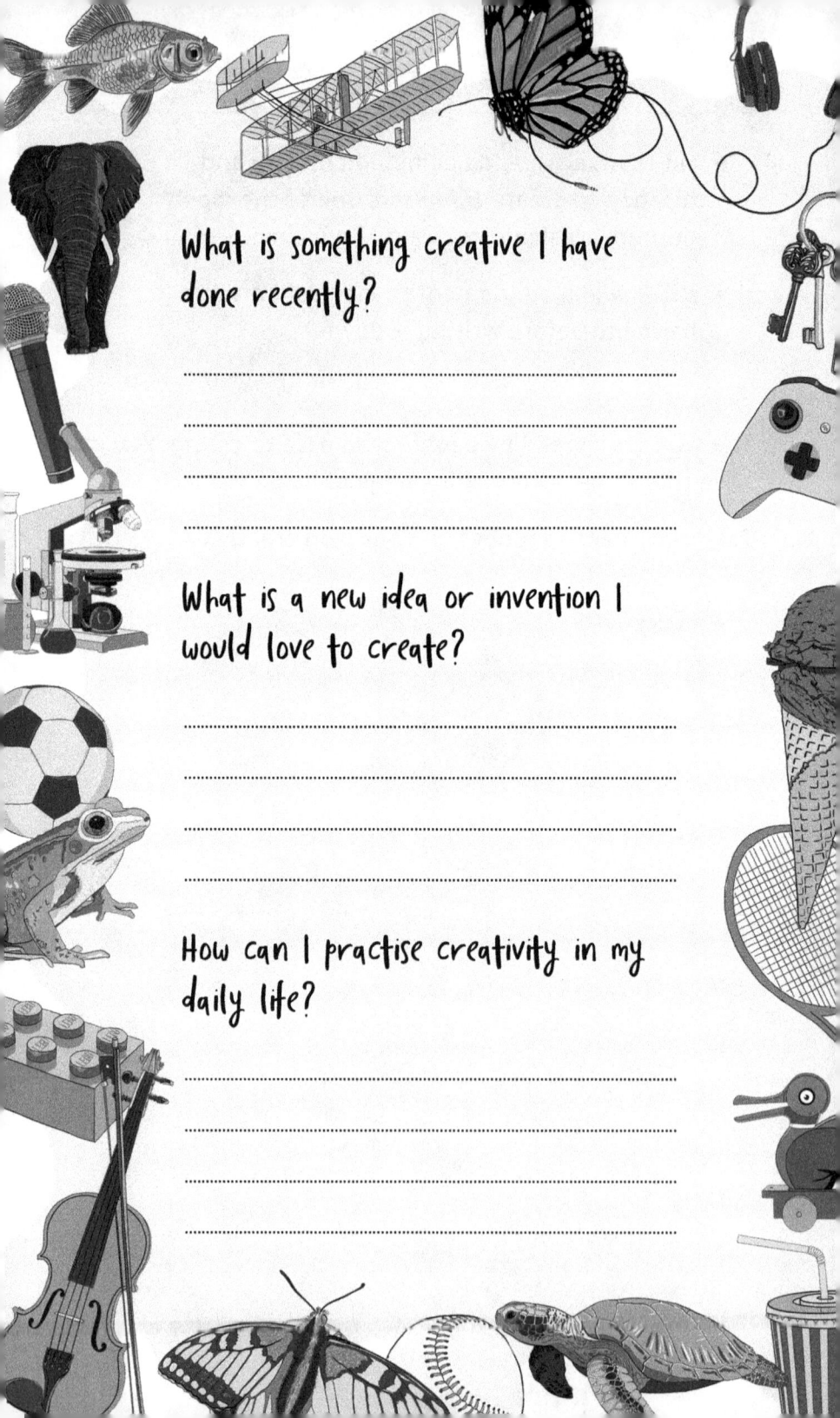

What is something creative I have done recently?

....

....

....

....

What is a new idea or invention I would love to create?

....

....

....

....

How can I practise creativity in my daily life?

....

....

....

....

A Lesson from the Greatest Creator

In the very beginning, before anything existed, God created the heavens and the earth. With just His voice, He spoke light into existence, separated the waters, shaped the land and filled the world with life. Everything we see – every tree, every star, every living creature – was created with intention and purpose.

And because we are made in His image, we have the ability to create, too!

In Matthew 25, Jesus tells the parable of the talents. A master gives three servants different amounts of money (talents) and then leaves on a journey. Two of the servants invest and multiply what they were given, but one buries his talent in the ground out of fear. When the master returns, he praises the first two for using what they were given and challenges the third for wasting his potential.

This story reminds us that creativity is a gift that we are meant to use, not hide away. Whether we create music, stories, inventions or new ways to solve problems, our creativity has the power to shape the world around us.

So, what will you create?

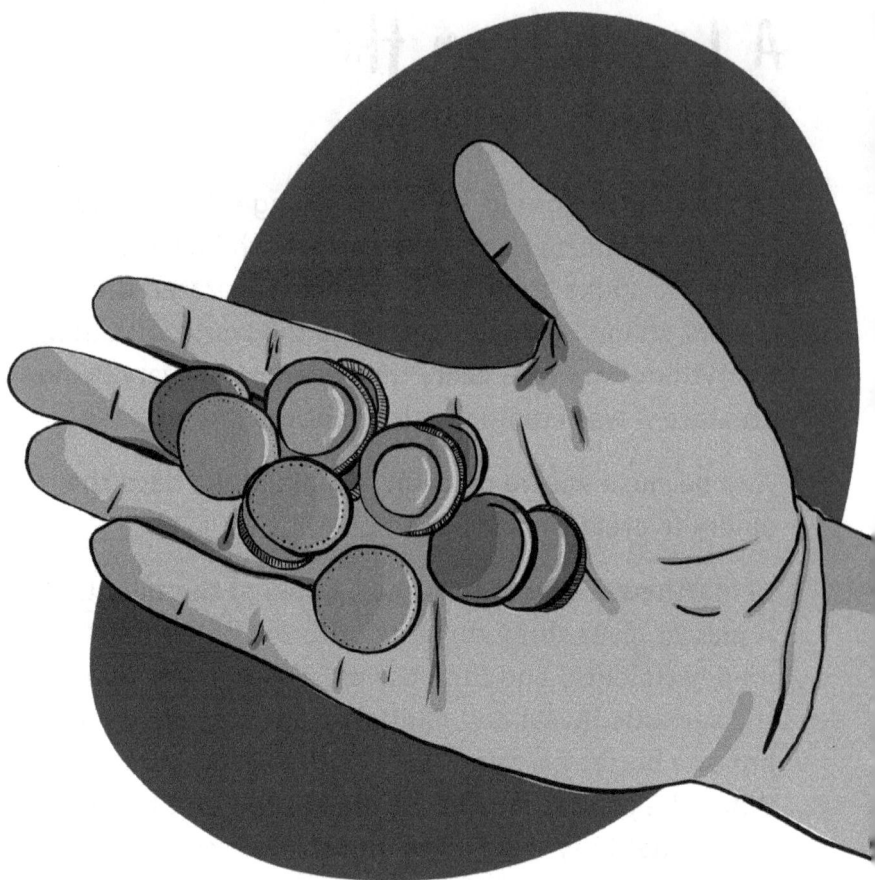

Spending Time In Nature

Have you ever noticed how being outside makes your mind feel full of ideas? Nature has a magical way of making us more creative! The sights, sounds and feelings of the outdoors can help us think in new ways, come up with fresh ideas and create amazing things. Here's how:

Nature is Beautiful!

From towering mountains to tiny raindrops on a flower, the world around us is bursting with beauty. Artists, writers and musicians often use nature to inspire their work. Have you ever seen a painting of a sunset or read a poem about the sea? That's because nature's beauty sparks our imagination!

Nature Helps Us Pay Attention

When we step outside, we start noticing things – like the way a butterfly flutters, how tree branches dance in the wind or how a bird sings its special song. The more we pay attention, the more ideas we have! Great storytellers, inventors and songwriters all know that looking closely at the world helps them create new things.

Nature Sparks Our Imagination

A floating cloud might look like a dragon. The rustling leaves might sound like whispers of a secret adventure. The waves at the beach might make you think of a song. The outdoors is like a giant playground for the imagination! Some of the most creative people in history got their best ideas from spending time in nature.

Nature Teaches Us Life Lessons

The changing seasons, the way plants grow and even the waves in the ocean can teach us important things about life. For example, trees lose their leaves in autumn but grow fresh new ones in spring – just like how we go through changes and grow in different ways!

Nature Helps Us Relax

Have you ever noticed how good it feels to take a deep breath of fresh air? Being outside can calm our minds, make us feel happy and give us space to think. When we're relaxed, we can come up with even better ideas! That's why so many artists, musicians and inventors take walks outside when they're looking for inspiration.

Nature Reminds Us of Something Bigger

Standing in front of a giant waterfall or looking up at a sky full of stars can make us feel amazed. Nature reminds us that

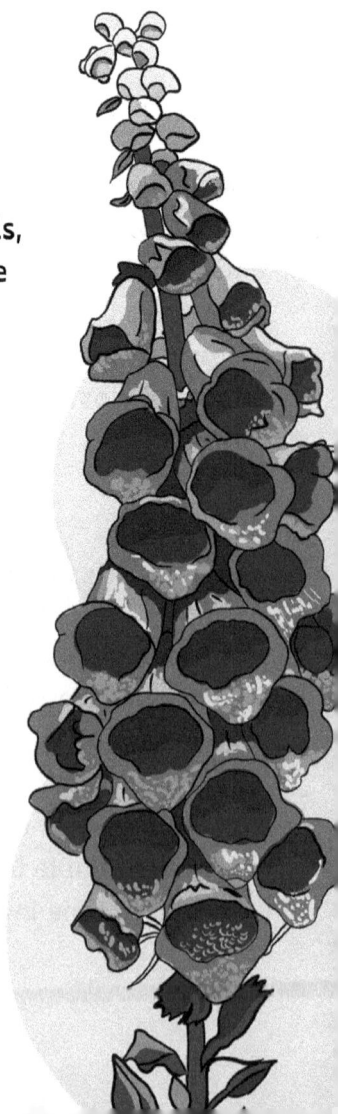

the world is full of wonder and possibilities. It makes us want to explore, discover and create something special to share with others!

So, how can YOU use nature to get creative?

- **Go outside and notice something new!** What's the most interesting shape, colour or sound you can find?

- **Make up a story inspired by nature!** What if a squirrel found a magical acorn? Or a raindrop had an exciting adventure?

- **Try drawing or painting something you see outside!** A tree? A cloud? A cool-looking rock?

Next time you're feeling stuck or out of ideas, step outside and see what nature has to offer. The world is full of inspiration – you just have to be curious enough to find it!

CHAPTER SIX

BE THE SPARK
Potential to...change

"Consult not your fears but your hopes and your dreams. Think not about your frustrations, but about your unfulfilled potential. Concern yourself not with what you tried and failed in, but with what it is still possible for you to do."

Pope John XXIII

Lena was upset.

"I just don't get why you're mad at me!" she said, crossing her arms.

Her best friend, Jordan, sighed. "Because, Lena, you promised we'd work on our science project together, but then you did half of it without me."

"I was just trying to help!" Lena protested. "We were behind schedule, so I thought I was making things easier for both of us."

Jordan shook his head. "But you didn't ask me. You just decided on your own. It made me feel like my ideas didn't matter."

Lena opened her mouth to argue, but then she paused. Had she ever thought about it that way?

"I wasn't trying to ignore your ideas," she said more softly. "I just thought you'd be happy I was getting things done."

Jordan shrugged. "I get that . . . but part of working together is making decisions together, too."

Lena thought about that. Maybe she had been so focused on getting the project done that she hadn't considered how Jordan felt.

"You're right," she admitted. "I should've talked to you first. I'm sorry."

Jordan smiled a little. "Thanks. And I probably overreacted, too. I know you were just trying to help."

Lena grinned. "So, truce?"

"Truce," Jordan agreed. "Now, let's actually finish this project – together this time."

Change Starts with Perspective

It's easy to believe we're right in the middle of a disagreement. But often, the real solution isn't about proving a point – it's about changing our perspective.

Change isn't just about the big things in life; sometimes, the most powerful change happens when we see a situation from someone else's point of view.

Have you ever had a disagreement where you later realised the other person had a good point?
What happened?

....
....
....
....

How did it feel when you tried to see things from their perspective?

....
....
....
....

What would you do differently next time?

....
....
....
....

The Power to Change is Always Yours

Sometimes, people get stuck believing that change is impossible. Maybe they've made mistakes in the past. Maybe others don't believe they can grow. Maybe **they** don't even believe it themselves.

But the truth is, **change is always possible.**

History is full of people who transformed their lives:

- **Abraham Lincoln** lost many elections before he became president.

- **Sir David Attenborough** started out as a TV producer but became one of the world's most respected voices for environmental change, inspiring millions to protect the planet.

- **Beyoncé** started as part of a girl group, but through years of reinvention, hard work and artistic vision, she became one of the most influential and ground-breaking artists of all time.

If they had listened to doubt, they would have stayed the same. But they **chose** to change.

No matter what others think or say, your potential to grow, improve and change **is yours alone**. You always have the power to take a new step, try again or see things in a new way.

So, what's something in your life that you want to change? And what's one small step you can take today to make it happen?

A Lesson from The Good Samaritan

One of the most famous stories about changing perspectives comes from a parable Jesus told – the story of the Good Samaritan.

A man was travelling when he was attacked by robbers and left injured on the road. A priest saw him but passed by. A religious leader saw him but walked away. But then, a Samaritan – someone from a group that was usually enemies with the man's people – stopped. He bandaged the man's wounds, took him to an inn, and paid for his care.

Jesus used this story to challenge people's perspectives on kindness. The ones who were expected to help didn't, but the one least expected to help was the one who showed compassion. The lesson? True change happens when we open our hearts and see others the way we would want to be seen.

Change isn't just about making things different – it's about making things better. And often, the first step to change is understanding.

Did You Know?

WOOD FROGS

Wood frogs have a special adaptation to survive the extreme cold that is common in winter in many of the places they inhabit. They allow themselves to become frozen! Well, not completely. Their bodies create a natural antifreeze that keeps ice from forming inside their partially frozen bodies. Ice crystals are very sharp and would damage their tissues and internal organs. When the weather warms up in the spring, they thaw out and become active again.

Your Potential is Endless

Throughout this book, we've explored the incredible power of **potential** – the ability to grow, learn and become more than we ever imagined.

- We saw how potential begins with **curiosity** and a willingness to explore new ideas.

- We learned that potential thrives when we **face challenges**, make mistakes and keep going.

- We discovered that potential isn't just about individual success – it's about **building upon what others have done** and creating something new.

- We found that our potential to **change** allows us to become better friends, better learners and better people.

No matter where you are in life, **you have potential.** Even when things feel difficult, even when others doubt you, even when you doubt yourself – your potential is still there, waiting to be unlocked.

So ask yourself:

What will I do with my potential? How will I use it to grow, to help others, to make a difference?

The answer is up to you.

Your journey is just beginning. And the possibilities are endless.

TO PARENTS AND TEACHERS:
Helping Young People Level Up

Dear Parents and Teachers,

Thank you for choosing the *Level Up* series to invest in the next generation. These books were written with a clear goal: to help young people discover and develop core values that will shape their lives from the inside out.

Each chapter is built around real-life stories, fun metaphors, faith-based inspiration and practical examples that children can relate to. To get the most out of these books, here are a few simple ways you can bring the content to life:

For Parents:

- **Bedtime conversations** – Read a chapter together and use it as a springboard for open, meaningful discussion.

- **Car chats** – Use chapter titles or questions as prompts during drives or while waiting in queues.

- **Celebrate growth** – When your child shows curiosity, confidence, respect or potential in action, call it out and cheer them on!

For Teachers:

- **Small group discussions** – Use chapters to spark class conversations, circle time or Personal/ Social/Health sessions.

- **Curriculum connections** – Many chapters link naturally with Religious Education, citizenship or literacy themes.

- **Creative response activities** – Invite students to write, draw or present their own take on a chapter's theme.

Whether you're reading with one child or a whole class, our hope is that these books will inspire a journey of growth – and give you the joy of walking that journey together.

Let's raise a generation ready to level up!

soul ⬟ children

SOUL CHILDREN UK :
Sing. Grow. Belong.

Do your children love to sing? Are you looking for a way to help them grow in confidence, creativity and community?

Soul Children UK is part of an international network of youth gospel choirs that gives children aged 9–16 a place to belong and a voice to be heard. Through high-energy rehearsals, powerful songs and inspiring performances, Soul Children helps young people discover who they are – and who they're becoming.

A message for teachers :

Thinking about starting a choir in your school or community? Soul Children UK provides everything you need:

- Songs kids love to sing

- Simple resources and support

- Training and encouragement for leaders

- A network of choirs across the UK – and beyond!

Whether you're a seasoned music teacher or just passionate about helping young people grow, you don't have to do it alone.

Visit soulchildrenuk.com to learn more, hear the music and join the movement.

worshiphouse KiDS

Ready to
SING, DANCE, AND DIVE
Deeper into Chip's Level Up Series?

Meet AAA – Access All Areas – the creative geniuses behind the songs, games, and all-out fun inspired by the values in Chip's book!

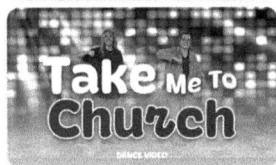

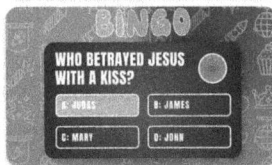

🎵 Jam out to kid-approved songs that bring the Bible to life

🕺 Dance your heart out with easy-to-follow videos

🎲 Play Bible Story Bingo & flex those Scripture smarts

📱 Scan that lil' QR code to explore the full collection on WorshipHouse Kids.

Let's keep **learning, laughing, and lifting** up His name—together (with some serious style, of course).

WANT CHIP TO VISIT YOUR SCHOOL OR CHURCH?

Hi, I'm Chip — author of the Level Up series. I love visiting schools and churches to talk about the values behind these books—things like confidence, potential, respect, and curiosity.

My sessions are packed with stories, games, real-life examples, and practical ways to live out what we learn. Sometimes I even bring my sound system and sing a song or two!

Whether it's for an assembly, classroom session, youth group, or Sunday service, I'd love to be part of what you're doing to inspire the next generation.

Want to find out more?

Email: bookings@chipkendall.com

Let's start the conversation!

READY FOR MORE?

You've reached the end of the book... ...but this is just the beginning of your Level Up journey!

Head over to levelupbooks.com to explore:

More Titles – Explore the rest of the Level Up series and find your next favourite book

Bonus Material – Activities, videos, downloads, and more to help you level up in real life

Bulk Purchase Offers – Perfect for schools, churches, and youth groups

Contact & Booking Info – Want Chip to visit your school or church? You'll find everything you need

Join the Mailing List – Be the first to hear about new releases, sneak peeks, and exclusive extras!

Let's keep growing, learning, and becoming the people we were made to be.

One choice at a time.
One level at a time.

Let's Level Up!

LEVEL UP
BOOKS

CHECK OUT THE FULL
LEVEL UP SERIES

The Courage Code – Level Up Your Confidence
ISBN 978-1-917455-30-5

The Silent Spark – Level Up Your Potential
ISBN 978-1-917455-27-5

The Echo Effect – Level Up Your Respect
ISBN 978-1-917455-28-2

The Wonder Switch – Level Up Your Curiosity
ISBN 978-1-917455-29-9

www.ingramcontent.com/pod-product-compliance
Lightning Source LLC
Chambersburg PA
CBHW060035050426
42448CB00012B/3026